BIRDS IN ART

William Henry Hunt (1790–1864), *White Hawthorn and Bird's Nest*.

BIRDS IN ART

Compiled by
FERDIE McDONALD

Introduction by Stephen Butler
Picture selection by Julia Brown

STUDIO EDITIONS
LONDON

This edition published 1994 by
Studio Editions Ltd
Princess House, 50 Eastcastle Street
London, W1N 7AP, England

Printed and bound in Singapore

ISBN 1 85891 177 X

INTRODUCTION

Above all other creatures, birds have assumed complex magical and symbolic functions in our attempts to understand the natural and supernatural worlds.

Since the earliest civilization, their apparent freedom has inspired both awe and envy in humans. Their songs, an impenetrable, secret language, seemed to express this freedom, and the creatures themselves came to represent the human spirit, the soul without the shackles of the body. The story of Icarus, whose waxen wings melted as he flew towards the Sun, embodies both our longing for freedom and the warning that we can never escape our earth-bound condition.

Once human society was established, individual species of bird played specific symbolic and mythological roles. Many such associations survive today, recurring across widely different cultures. The owl still symbolizes wisdom as it did in ancient Greece; the fabulous phoenix represents renewal and rebirth from the Sahara to China (*see* Plate 4); the eagle signifies nobility as it did to the Romans; the raven means death as it did in Celtic times.

Having the freedom of the air, birds were often thought to be bringers of messages from the gods, and thus gained prophetic and oracular associations. Linked with this idea, certain species have become harbingers of death; the owl, raven, jackdaw, and, in the United States, the whippoorwill have all assumed this role. Surprisingly, perhaps, the vulture was associated with medicine and healing by the Greeks.

Today the most potent and widely understood bird symbol is undoubtedly the dove. As the bringer of good news to Noah (*see* Plate 1), the symbol of love to the psalmist and the embodiment of the Holy Spirit in thousands of New Testament images, its transformation into a symbol of international peace has been a natural progression. There is indeed a long-established tradition of dove- and pigeon-painting, to which Picasso has most famously contributed.

Birds have long been used for purely decorative purposes as well as for their symbolic associations. In western medieval manuscripts they were

French illuminated manuscript, fifteenth century (detail). Depictions of real and mythological birds and animals were often included in illuminated manuscripts.

Hans Hoffman (*d. c.* 1591), *The Wing of a European Roller*. Hoffman was inspired by the works of Albrecht Dürer, hence this copy of Dürer's 1512 original of the same title.

often employed in just such simple terms, appearing as fantastic creations with superb plumage. As this tradition grew more sophisticated, however, artists began to depict species in precise detail. This was equally evident in Far Eastern Art, where the ancient tradition of scroll illustration and the nineteenth-century skill of printing on silk and paper produced many vivid bird images, combining accuracy with verve.

As the European Renaissance progressed, there developed a northern tradition of still life, in which animals and birds — especially game-birds — were displayed alongside flowers, fruit and vegetables, as symbols of mankind's God-given domination over bountiful nature. Here, the aim was to achieve the highest degree of realism, and the artists were more concerned with the mechanics and effect of the picture than with the creatures themselves, which were, in any case, usually shown dead. However, the close observation such subjects required led to some extraordinarily detailed works. Two pictures from that period are interesting consequences of this tradition: Albrecht Dürer's *Wing of a European Roller* and Carel Fabritius's *Goldfinch* (*see* Plate 6). These were exercises rather than commercial paintings, but display the same stringent concern for accuracy.

THAUMALEA PICTA

Joseph Wolf (1820–99), *Golden Pheasant*. Wolf's mastery of bird art is evident in this impressive illustration from Daniel Giraud Elliot's *Monograph of the Phasianidae*, 1872.

The still life gradually shed many of its religious and symbolic overtones, and became increasingly contrived and decorative, as in the work of Melchior Hondecoeter (*see* Plates 7 & 8). Meanwhile, world exploration brought evermore gorgeous and exotic specimens to embellish the genre.

With the dawning of the scientific age in the eighteenth century, art became more widely available through engravings. At the same time, the new sciences demanded a precise and inclusive cataloguing of species. The ornithologist and engraver Thomas Bewick (1753–1828) is regarded as the founder of 'scientific' natural history illustration, which developed into the great nineteenth-century tradition of John James Audubon, John Gould, Archibald Thorburn and Edward Lear (*see* Plates 12 & 14). These painters were required to combine absolute accuracy and technical competence with aesthetic composition. Their example will perhaps never be surpassed, though the tradition remains a strong one, with a dedicated following of artists, collectors and scholars.

Although birds continued to appear in genre paintings, such as William Leech's *Goose Girl* (*see* Plate 22), they regained their symbolic value in modern times, as artists began to represent our inner as well as our external life. The Symbolists and Surrealists frequently used birds as personal or mythological symbols. Max Ernst (1891–1976) depicted what he saw as their terrifying power and sexual significance; and Marc Chagall (1887–1985), in creating his fantastic, floating visions, turned to Jewish folk-tales, which abounded with images of cockerels and other birds with magical associations. Other twentieth-century painters, such as Graham Sutherland and C W R Nevinson, have continued the tradition of using birds in essentially decorative contexts.

Chagall himself saw painting as 'a window through which I could have taken flight to another world.' For as long as human beings are seekers after freedom, we will aspire to share the airy kingdom of the birds, and artists will continue to capture them in all their magnificence and mystery.

— THE —
PLATES

PLATE 1

Basilica di San Marco, Venice
Mosaic (13th century)

Noah sends out the Dove from the Ark

DETAIL

Go, beautiful and gentle dove,
  And greet the morning ray;
For lo! the sun shines bright above,
  And night and storm are pass'd away:
No longer drooping, here confin'd,
  In this cold prison dwell;
Go, free to sunshine and to wind,
  Sweet bird, go forth, and fare-thee-well.

From *The Dove from the Ark*
WILLIAM LISLE BOWLES (1762–1850)

PLATE 2

Giotto (*c.* 1266−1337)

St Francis of Assisi Preaching to the Birds

DETAIL

... a number of swallows who were building their nests nearby, began to twitter loudly and to make such a noise, that Blessed Francis could not be heard by the people.

Then he addressed the birds as follows: "Swallows, my sisters, it is now time that I should speak, you have said enough! Listen to the word of the Lord, be silent and keep quiet until the sermon is over!" And to the amazement of those who stood around, the swallows fell silent at once and did not move from the spot until the sermon was at an end.

From *The Life of St Francis of Assisi*
THOMAS of CELANO (*c.* 1190–1260)

PLATE 3

Benozzo Gozzoli (*c.*1421–97)

Falcon with Dead Hare

DETAIL

"Call down the hawk from the air;
Let him be hooded or caged
Till the yellow eye has grown mild,
For larder and spit are bare,
The old cook enraged,
The scullion gone wild."

"I will not be clapped in a hood,
Nor a cage, nor alight upon wrist,
Now I have learnt to be proud
Hovering over the wood
In the broken mist
Or tumbling cloud."

From *The Hawk*
W B YEATS (1865–1939)

PLATE 4

Historia Naturalis (*c.*1460)
Italian Manuscript

Phoenix on Nest
DETAIL

When the sun comes up from the salt sea,
That radiant bird, in all his brightness,
Flies from his branch in the forest tree,
And moves in swift winged flight through the air,
Singing melodious songs to the sun.
The phoenix's voice is surpassing fair,
Inspired by his spirit's blissful joy.

From *The Phoenix*
ANON

EO V
auium
dissim
rum q
meli a
ci alt
msider
dunt
Adhoc
penni
aduut
sunt
terra
his ce
mica
prehe

utiles: quos in fuga contra sequentes ingerunt pedib
dilectu deuorata mira natura: sed non minus stol

PLATE 5

Jean Jacques Walter (*c.* 1600–77)

Study of a Lapwing

O Lapwing, thou fliest around the heath,
Nor seest the net that is spread beneath.
Why dost thou not fly among the cornfields?
They cannot spread nets where a harvest yields.

O Lapwing
WILLIAM BLAKE (1757–1827)

Vanellus Ein Kibitz

PLATE 6

Carel Fabritius (1622–54)

The Goldfinch

DETAIL

Sometimes goldfinches one by one will drop
From low hung branches; little space they stop;
But sip, and twitter, and their feathers sleek;
Then off at once, as in a wanton freak:
Or perhaps, to show their black and golden wings,
Pausing upon their yellow flutterings.

From *I Stood Tip-Toe*
JOHN KEATS (1795–1821)

PLATE 7

Melchior Hondecoeter (1636−95)

Landscape with Birds
DETAIL

The silver swan, who living had no note,
When death approached unlocked her silent throat;
Leaning her breast against the reedy shore,
Thus sung her first and last, and sung no more:
Farewell, all joys; O death, come close mine eyes;
More geese than swans now live, more fools than wise.

ANON

PLATE 8

Melchior Hondecoeter (1636−95)

A Peacock on a Decorative Urn

The bird itself is a thing of beauty, supreme in this respect among living
forms, therefore, as we have seen, the symbol in art of all that
is highest in the spiritual world.

From *Adventures Among Birds*
WILLIAM HENRY HUDSON (1841−1922)

PLATE 9

Carl Wilhelm de Hamilton (1668–1754)

The Parliament of Birds

For this was on seynt Valentynes day,
Whan every foul cometh ther to chese his make,
Of every kinde, that men thenke may;
And that so huge a noyse gan they make,
That erthe and see, and tree, and every lake
So ful was, that unnethe was ther space
For me to stonde, su ful was al the place.

From *The Parlement of Foules*
GEOFFREY CHAUCER (*c.* 1343–1400)

PLATE 10

Aert Schouman (1710−92)

A Great White Crested Cockatoo

DETAIL

I should say they were the noisiest birds in the bush; their deplorable voices are not in the least in keeping with the glorious white of their bodies seen against the green of ancient gums. "Spirits of light" the explorer Mitchell called them, and rightly; but their note is as the crackling of thorns under the pot.

From *Birds of the District of Geelong*
CHARLES F BELCHER (1876−1970)

PLATE 11

J M W Turner (1775–1851)

Heron with Fish in Mouth

Getting a little more into the stream, he stands a few moments, again advances, then with body projecting, horizontally, on either side of the legs—like the head of a mallet—and neck a little outstretched, he stops once more. At once he makes a dart forward, so far forward that he almost—nay, sometimes quite—overbalances, the neck shoots out as from a spring, and instantly he has a fair-sized fish in his bill, which, after a little tussling and quiet insistence—gone through like a grave formal etiquette—he swallows.

From *Bird Life Glimpses*
EDMUND SELOUS (1857–1934)

PLATE 12

John James Audubon (1785–1851)

Roseate Spoonbill

To procure their food, the Spoonbills first generally alight near the water, into which they then wade up to the tibia, and immerse their bills in the water or soft mud, sometimes with the head and even the whole neck beneath the surface. They frequently withdraw these parts however, and look around to ascertain if danger is near. They move their partially opened mandibles laterally to and fro with a considerable degree of elegance, munching the fry, insects, or small shell-fish, which they secure, before swallowing them.

From *American Ornithological Biography*
JOHN JAMES AUDUBON (1785–1851)

PLATE 13

Ando Hiroshige (1797−1858)

Eagle Over Susaki

DETAIL

He clasps the crag with crooked hands;
Close to the sun in lonely lands,
Ringed with the azure world, he stands.

The wrinkled sea beneath him crawls;
He watches from his mountain walls,
And like a thunderbolt he falls.

The Eagle
ALFRED, LORD TENNYSON (1809−92)

PLATE 14

John Gould (1804–1881)
Song Thrush

Within a thick and spreading hawthorn bush,
That overhung a mole-hill large and round,
I heard from morn to morn a merry thrush
Sing hymns of rapture, while I drank the sound
With joy—and oft, an unintruding guest,
I watched her secret toils from day to day;
How true she warped the moss to form her nest,
And modelled it within with wood and clay,
And by and by, like heath-bells gilt with dew,
There lay her shining eggs as bright as flowers,
Ink-spotted over, shells of green and blue:
And there I witnessed in the summer hours
A brood of nature's minstrels chirp and fly,
Glad as the sunshine and the laughing sky.

The Thrush's Nest
JOHN CLARE (1793–1864)

PLATE 15

Harrison William Weir (1824–1906)

The Kingfisher's Haunt

It was the Rainbow gave thee birth,
   And left thee all her lovely hues;
And, as her mother's name was Tears,
   So runs it in my blood to choose
For haunts the lonely pools, and keep
In company with trees that weep.

From *The Kingfisher*
WILLIAM HENRY DAVIES (1871–1940)

PLATE 16

James Bourhill (*fl.*1880−87)

Pouter Pigeons

I do not hesitate to affirm that some domestic races of the rock-pigeon differ fully as much from each other in external characters as do the most distinct natural genera. We may look in vain through the 288 known species for a beak so small and conical as that of the short-faced tumbler; for one so broad and short as that of the barb; for one so long, straight, and narrow, with its enormous wattles, as that of the English carrier; for an expanded upraised tail like that of the fantail; or for an oesophagus like that of the pouter.

From *The Variation of Animals and Plants under Domestication*
CHARLES DARWIN (1809−82)

PLATE 17

Eloise Harriet Stannard (1829–1915)

Still Life with Strawberries and Bluetits

Where is he, that giddy sprite,
Blue-cap, with his colours bright,
Who was blest as bird could be,
Feeding in the apple tree;
Made such wanton spoil and rout,
Turning blossoms inside out:
Hung – head pointing towards the ground –
Fluttered, perched, into a round
Bound himself, and then unbound;
Littlest, gaudiest Harlequin!
Prettiest tumbler ever seen!

From *The Kitten and Falling Leaves*
WILLIAM WORDSWORTH (1770–1850)

PLATE 18

John Wainwright (1855–1931)

Primrose and Robin
DETAIL

Goodbye, goodbye to summer!
  For summer's nearly done;
The garden smiling faintly,
  Cool breezes in the sun;
Our thrushes now are silent,
  Our swallows flown away –
But Robin's here, in coat of brown,
  With ruddy breast-knot gay.
Robin, Robin Redbreast,
  O Robin dear!
Robin sings so sweetly
  In the falling of the year.

From *Robin Redbreast*
WILLIAM ALLINGHAM (1824–89)

PLATE 19

Joseph Crawhall (1861–1913)

A Duck in a Meadow

I remember some years ago when strolling by the Itchen I stood to admire a white duck floating on the clear current where it is broad and shallow and where the flowering wild musk was abundant. The rich moist green of the plant made the white plumage seem whiter, and the flowers and the duck's beak were both a very beautiful yellow.

From *Adventures Among Birds*
WILLIAM HENRY HUDSON (1841–1922)

PLATE 20

Joseph Crawhall (1861–1913)

The Spangled Cock

I sometimes think I'd rather crow
And be a rooster than to roost
And be a crow. But I dunno.

A rooster he can roost also,
Which don't seem fair when crows can't crow.
Which may help some. Still I dunno.

Crows should be glad of one thing, though;
Nobody thinks of eating crow,
While roosters they are good enough
For anyone unless they're tough.

There are lots of tough old roosters though,
And anyway a crow can't crow,
So mebby roosters stand more show,
It looks that way. But I dunno.

To Be or Not to Be
ANON

PLATE 21

Koson (1877−1945)

An Owl on a Tree Branch
DETAIL

Come, doleful owl, the messenger of woe,
   Melancholy's bird, companion of despair,
Sorrow's best friend, and mirth's professèd foe,
   The chief discourser that delights sad care.
O come, poor owl, and tell thy woes to me,
Which having heard, I'll do the like for thee.

ANON

PLATE 22

William Leech (1881–1968)

The Goose Girl

Goosey goosey gander,
Whither shall I wander?
Upstairs and downstairs
And in my lady's chamber.

Goosey Goosey Gander
NURSERY RHYME

PLATE 23

Ethleen Palmer (*fl*. 1930–40)

Hornbills

The hornbills, though less beautiful than the toucans, are more curious, from the strange forms of their huge bills, which are often adorned with ridges, knobs, or recurved horns. They are bulky and heavy birds, and during flight beat the air with prodigious force, producing a rushing sound very like the puff of a locomotive, and which can sometimes be heard a mile off.

From *Natural Selection and Tropical Nature*
ALFRED RUSSELL WALLACE (1823–1913)

PLATE 24

Charles Tunnicliffe (1901−79)

A Group of Ringed Plovers on the Sea Shore

...but yet lives there the man, calling himself an ornithologist, who, quietly strolling along the bright sandy beach just left bare by the retiring tide, and aroused from his pleasing reveries by the mellow whistle of the Ring-Plover, would not gaze with delight on the pleasant little thing that speeds away before him with twinkling feet, now stops, pipes its clear cry, runs, spreads its beautiful wings, glides close over the sand, and alights on some not distant tuft.

From *A History of British Birds*
WILLIAM MacGILLIVRAY (1796−1852)

PLATE 25

Carl Donner (*b.* 1957)

Pheasants in Flight

See! from the brake the whirring pheasant springs,
And mounts exulting on triumphant wings:
Short is his joy; he feels the fiery wound,
Flutters in blood, and panting beats the ground.
Ah! what avail his glossy, varying dyes,
His purple crest, and scarlet-circled eyes,
The vivid green his shining plumes unfold,
His painted wings, and breast that flames with gold?

From *Windsor Forest*
ALEXANDER POPE (1688–1744)